THE FEATHERED HEART

I love to go wandering
out among the trees,
to listen to them whisper
as the wind blows through their leaves.

D.M. Demery

THE FEATHERED HEART

by Mark Turcotte

Michigan State University Press
East Lansing

Copyright 1995, 1998 by Mark Andrew Turcotte

Michigan State University Press
East Lansing, Michigan 48823-5202

03 02 00 99 98 1 2 3 4 5 6 7 8 9

Library of Congress Cataloging-in-Publication Data

Turcotte, Mark.
    the feathered heart / Mark Turcotte
        p.   cm. -- (Native American series)
    ISBN 0-87013-482-5 (alk. paper)
    I. Title. II. Series: Native American series
    (East Lansing, Mich.)
    PS3570.U627F4 1998
    811'.54--dc21   98-23119
                                               CIP

Some of the poems in this collection first appeared
in the following publications: *Dark Night field notes*,
Hammers, *Hyphen Magazine*, and *The Eagle*.

A version of the poem *Animal Shadows* first appeared as text for a
pen and ink drawing, *Ceremony*, by artist Jeff Abbey Maldonado.

A first edition of *The Feathered Heart* was published by
MARCH/Abrazo Press, Chicago, in April 1995

Cover Art: *Two Worlds Hand*, by the author.
Illustrations: Kathleen S. Presnell
Design: Michael M. Smith

Michigan State University Press Native American Series
Native American Series Editor: Clifford E. Trafzer

Acknowledgments

Love and grace to my family, the old and new tribe.

Thanks to Vernon Blackdog Lee, Michael Warr and
the Guild Complex, Faith Attaguile and all the Dark Night
Relatives (Free Leonard Peltier), Mick Vranich and Sherry Hendrick,
S.K. Power, Quraysh Ali and Emily Hooper Lansana, Glenda Baker,
Kimberly Blaeser, Shana Mandel, R. Russell, Marc Smith,
Yorke Corbin, Carlos Cortez, Susan Power, Mike Puican,
Ray Gonzalez, Dee Sweet, Tracye Matthews, Mitar Mitch Covic,
Beryl and Gene Zitch.

More love and grace to Bobbie Pankratz, Suzanne Frank,
Loyal Suntken and Jim Mottonen for the many years of
friendship and patience.

The Feathered Heart
is dedicated to

my mother,
Dorothea Marie

Patti Smith and PSG,
whose words and music
saved my life
and showed me
the sea of possibilities

and

my wife, Kathleen,
who has given
all.

Contents

Introduction

As Native American literature reaches new levels of accomplishment, poets like Mark Turcotte will emerge and redefine everything we have known about this vibrant genre. *The Feathered Heart* proves the deepest and most personal memories are entryways into the poetic spirit that has shaped Native writing for the past century. Turcotte's poems arise from this tradition, but they clearly gain new ground in the consciousness that pulls our most vital poets together. Reading these poems means any notions about Native Writing can be left behind. There are ghosts here, but they do not haunt us because of our national history. They come alive in these poems because Turcotte's voice demands we look behind us to see what we have missed. By reading them, we gain strength for the next century. There is love and bitterness here, but they pass through the stream of the heart and mind any poet crosses when language demands these forces come alive.

Most important of all, there is dark hope and proud vision in the poems of *The Feathered Heart*. Turcotte knows which words bring us to these doors and he writes as if his chest is about to break open in song and wisdom. The short, lyrical chant and the longer meditative poem are reshaped by Turcotte's ability to find union with his tribal past, his childhood experiences, and the need to survive in modern America. The result is a first book of poems that will not allow itself to be labeled as just another book of Native American writing. There is a restless and magnetic music here and its capacity to make us look at hearts increases with each reading.

The Feathered Heart is a revelation and a bridge to the next century. After the enormous changes that have overtaken U.S. literature in the last decade, the idea of a true multicultural writing must be replaced by a more genuine poetics of culture and universal character. Turcotte's poems move us in this new direction with their ability to transform his personal world into timeless moments of transcendence. At the end of the book, we know what he knows and we see what he sees. Yet, the surprises in these poems never end. Their magic and their way of drawing the reader closer means a new kind of writing is being created. It is shaped with a language that prepares us for the future direction of a genuine American poetry. *The Feathered Heart* proves the next century is the fertile ground where Native voices are the first to pronounce there is a new vision and it is granting us the gift of poetry.

Ray Gonzalez

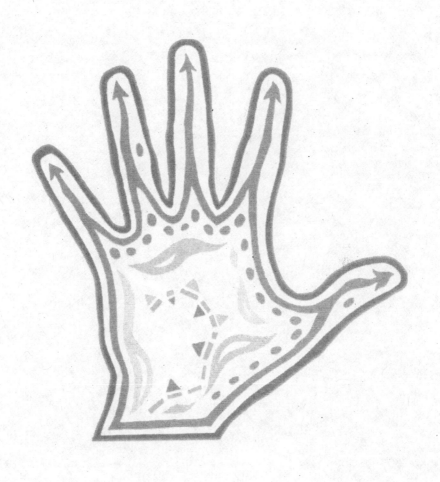

The Eye Shakes

I'm trying to remember what I do not remember.
Images come in stuttering phrases, staccato, bent
and broken, as if seen through the spokes of a
madly spinning wheel. Flickering black and white
clatters into color. The eye begins to shake, not
wanting to remember.

Images . . . images . . . images.

The rusted bed of a speeding pick-up truck. Two
children hunkered down, hiding. A boy and a girl.
Gravel spatters the underside of the truck. The
boy lifts his head, peers over the tailgate. A car is
following, one headlight shining. The boy sees,
faintly, the Devil, crouching upon the hood of the
car, laughing. The eye begins to shake.

Horse and Cradle

for Dorothea Marie

She, white woman, fell
in love with the
black wave
of his hair, with
the way his
voice rose up out of him
    from the Earth, the way
his flirtatious hands fell
over the strings of his guitar.

She fell, white woman,
in love with the
points of his eyes, the soft
circles they cut
through her shoulders, with
the way that he
came to her bed dressed
in savage feathers,
her bed, where
she climbed upon his
copperbrown
horse of a back, where
she carried the arrow in
her heart, she
became my mother,
the gently, ever gently
rocking cradle
of my soul.

Tiny Warriors

Whose voice was first sounded on this land?

Mahpiya Luta (Red Cloud)

Jesse and me, we little boys,
prance the top of the hill,
galloping
our wind horses
through the tall grass whispering
low across our
brown backs.

The voice of centuries
murmurs old tongues,
forgotten in our ears,
familiar
to the feather in our hearts,
remembered
in the frenzy of our blood.

The voice of centuries
spins sacred sunlight song
upon our heads,
beneath our heels and
we laughing, leaping
tiny warriors
ride and fall and ride and fall,
we ride
and all fall down the hill,

the whispers fading,

the skin of our chests
stretched tight
over heaving *Ojibway* drums.

3

Flies Buzzing

somewhere in america, in a certain state of grace . . .
Patti Smith

As a child I danced
to the heartful, savage
rhythm
of the Native, the
American Indian,
in the Turtle Mountains,
in the Round Hall,
in the greasy light of
kerosene lamps.

As a child I danced
among the long, jangle legs of
the men, down
    beside the whispering moccasin women,
in close circles
around the Old Ones,
who sat at the drum,
their heads tossed, backs arched
    in ancient prayer.

As a child I danced away from the fist,
I danced toward the rhythm of life,
I danced into dreams, into
    the sound of flies buzzing.
A deer advancing but clinging to the forest wall,
the old red woman rocking in her tattered shawl,
the young women bent, breasts
drooping to the mouths of their young, the heat
hanging heavy on the tips of our tongues,

until the Sun
burned the sky black, the moon
made us silvery blue and
all of the night sounds, all of the night sounds

folded together with the buzzing
still in our heads,
becoming a chant of ghosts,
of *Crazy Horse* and *Wovoka*
and all the endless Others,
snaking through the weaving through the trees
like beams of ribbons of light,
    singing, *we shall live again we shall live,*

until the Sun and the Sun and the Sun and I
awaken,
still a child, still dancing
toward the rhythm of life.

True Sign

He was
the first of all of them
in his Sunday school class
to memorize the "Lord's Prayer,"
the first to mumble,
    go to Hell,
as he slumped in a pew
beside his mother.

He knew
it wasn't right, all of this
combing his hair, tucking
in his shirt tail,
saving his dimes
for the collection plate,
getting down
upon his knees
to pray.

So he
would lie on his back
in the summer grass
of late Sunday morning
and he
would watch
the sky
for a true sign,

a hawk
arching toward the Sun,
loosing a feather,
    floating falling,
to land upon his bare brown chest.

Indian Boys

One little
two little
three little
four little
five little
six little
seven little
eight little
nine little
ten little.

Under the moon,
that perfect ruby sky fruit,
Indian boys pace
or carve through the nightness
in rusted cars,
their thick lips
wetted, glistening
with the breath of sick roses
and bad wine,

while one sad feather swings
upside down
from the rearview mirror,
brushing
Catholic dust from
the head of a cracked
    and yellow
dashboard Madonna.

Room Still Full of Death

A flame
within a lamp,
upon a table,
against the wall,
below a clock,
dripping time
onto the floor,
where shadows shake
the smell of Earth
from the boots
of the man,
as he listens
to the moan
of longing
from the corner
that is dark,

and he whispers, harshly,

sleep child,
your mother
is lying deep.

Father's Dust

The child was struck
at a tender age
with
the dry-mouth taste
of his father's dust,

dust of lies,
dust of rage,
dust of wandering,
dust of going away,

then finally,
the dust of never returning.

The child was struck,
gasping for air,
parched,
left choking
on the memory
growing in his throat.

For his father
made the Earth shudder
beneath the fall
of his foot,
for his father
made men tremble
beneath the gust
of his voice,

for his father
ate the sky
with his teeth

and
with his hands
dragged deep scars
into the flesh
of hearts
of backs
of minds
into the flesh
of dreams,

for his father
was the first
to bruise the child
with the fist of impatience,
for his father
was the first
to rape the child
with the body of shame,
for his father
was the first
to sting the child
with the tongue of hate.

The child was struck
at a tender age
with
the dry-mouth taste
of his father's dust,

for his father
was the first
to make the child
want to spit.

Window Glass

for Bobbie

He often found himself,
late at night,
looking
to the skies,
    imagining the stars
as razors
scraping up against the
blackness, as if
it were all just a painted-over
    window glass and
somewhere beyond there was another light.

Unshadow

And he dreamed of another light.

Another light
that would not fall
in shafts or rays
but instead be
carried curved
on the wind
into all our darkest places.

A light on the wind into
every crack of
every street of
every house of
every room, into
every dimly known corner
of every heart.

A light of anger grace
and healing
curving on the wind
to unshadow all those mouths
filled with all those tiny whisperings,
curving on the wind
to unshadow all those eyes
filled with all those tiny visions.

A light of anger grace
and healing
curving on the wind
to unshadow all those rough hands
filled with every unwanted touch,
curving on the wind
to unshadow all those rough words
filled with every unneeded cut.

A light of anger grace
and healing
curving on the wind
to unshadow every muffled refusal
    every defiled trust
    every stony denial,
curving on the wind
to unshadow every shadow.

And as he dreamed
he felt,
over his shoulder,
the wind
beginning to shine.

Sky Breathes Sky

Earth woman I
am made
of you,
the strong clay
of you
builds my bones,
   the soft clay,

the milk
of you
falls in light
   from my eyes.

Earth woman,
your river rushes blood
in my hands, rushes
in my hips,
   filling me,

your sky breathes sky breathes
of me,
your fire
lives on my voice,
   whispers.

Earth woman,
the wind
of you
sighs, rises
   in my soul,

the skin
of you
feathers my heart, the bird
in my chest,

that sings
at the scent sight
   of you.

Earth woman I
am blessed,
    made of you.

Flying With the Wind

for Cyrus

He is gone into the dust,
    flying with the wind
over the turtle-backed hills
into the far and the far and the far.

He is gone
into the trees,
into the black earth,
into the thick grass
beneath my belly,
where I am
stretched out,
cradling the pipe
and remembering him.

His gnarled, beadworking fingers
are gone,
his squinting gaze
gone,
his crooked mouth,
his brittle bones
and their creaking
whenever he walked,
whenever he reached
    to scratch his scalp
with a stiff, stubborn thumb.

Flying with the wind,
his trembling voice
is gone,
his clicking Cree tongue,
his laughter
gone,
with his wise heart

and its ever-expanding embrace,

and I roll over, I stand
to the rising Sun,
I light the pipe and I lift it
to the highest point
    of the empty yellow sky.

Flying with the wind,
he is gone
but for one puff
    of smoke from somewhere.

Horse Dance

I do not know where these words come from,
it is the only way I can speak.

Mike Puican

We dream
the pony of Crazy Horse
twisting
in a field
of yellow hair,
its nervous neck
painted with
a hail of stones,
    stomp
    step step
    stomp
    step step.

We dream
the pony of Crazy Horse
dancing
in a field
of greasy grass,
polishing its anxious hooves
upon the buttons
of Custer's coat,
    stomp
    step step
    stomp.

We dream
the pony of Crazy Horse
leaping
in a field
of horses grazing,
riderless,

deaf to the distant wail of a widow
crying,
why my Georgie, why my Georgie why,
    stomp.

We dream
the pony of Crazy Horse
rising
in a field
of bloodied flowers,
where the horn
of her husband's empty saddle
is still decorated
with the flesh of Lakota women,
that is *why my Georgie why,*
    stomp
    step step
    step step . . .

Recognize Stepfather

Years later,
after we
escaped you
and the reservation,
I was seventeen, strong
and still
very angry,
and I was visiting there,
when I recognized
you.

I recognized you immediately,
stumbling
from another barroom door,
I recognized you immediately,
leaning upon the wall,
swaying toward me
and I recognized, immediately,
that I
was going to kill you.

Because I remembered it all,
I remembered all of it.

The little boy,
standing on
the straw-filled
mattress screaming, with
each click
of your fist
upon his mother's jaw,

the little boy,
with your boot bottomed
against his neck,

smashing his face
into the dirt floor,

the little boy,
trying really trying
not to
let you
see him cry,

the little boy,
covering his head trying
not to listen to
the *no no no Daddy*
from his big sister,

the little boy,
begging God just
to take
you away,
then promising to do it
himself, someday.

Because I remembered it all,
I remembered all of it.

And I recognized you
as you slipped,
as my heart blackened,
and I recognized you
as you fell,
as my hands balled into fists,

and I recognized myself
rushing upon you,
yanking you up
by the collar, baring my teeth,
ready to break you in half,

when I recognized
that you were too limp,
that you were too weak,
that you were too broken
    to break.

So, I carried you across the street
into the warmth
of a late-night laundromat,
propped you up
in a chair,
dabbed your spitty mouth
with my sleeve,
and I
went back outside
and I

tried I really tried
not to cry.

And Betty Jean

He came back quietly,
crooked, his face
longer, the deep green jungle
sweating from his eyes.

He came back falling,
fingers pushing through
his hair, covering
his ears.

And Betty Jean Betty Jean
found him in the darkness
of their motel room.
But she could not reach
him anymore,
could not feel him anymore,

even when he was inside,
    when he left himself inside,
could not feel him anymore,
even when he took the gun
and sucked
the bullets out.

And Betty Jean Betty Jean
she said she missed him so
    she missed him so.
And Betty Jean Betty Jean
she told us that he never came back.
She pushed her fingers through
her hair, covering
her ears
and told us he never.

Under Gray Gods

I have seen for some time now the change in everything.
Rainer Maria Rilke

Fall into autumn,
where the hours lay cold
in the thin branches
and the leaves all scatter,
erasing the ground,
to pillow
against the fences lining
the fields.

I rest in the Earth,
in the furrows, the folds,
while
the plowers circle
and smoke the sky.

Here, time is my breathing my breath
is slow,
and I'm praying
to vanish
into the gray Gods dancing
in front of my eyes.

Folded Down

I remember it was
winter and
my hair was
longer than it had ever been.

We were together in the basement,
with that sweet smoky juice
invading our veins,
and I remember
the ember reflecting in
her eye.

Some sound some sound was
waving at me
from two dark corners
and, when I reached
to open her, she
    folded around my fingers,
folded down
to the floor,
as the ember dimmed away.

I remember it was, and
my hair was, and
I leaned back into the wall,
took a ride
on the elastic train of thought,
it lasted all night and
then some.

Animal Shadows

Nuevos amantes Indios
rise together
on a motel bed.

Drenched in pink
and blue neon,
their shadows
spill across the floor.

Sweat purples down her back, flames
across his chest,
throwing silhouettes.
    Wings teeth paws
appear upon the wall.

She bites her lip, closes
her eyes.
He turns to a breath
at his neck,

antlers tangle in her hair.

Indio

I was El Indio,
the night of the dance.
Down along the border whirling,
    I watched her whirl to Tejano guitars,
while golden, beckoning birds
flew from beneath her shimmering skirt.

My tequila fingers,
reaching for her,
trapped a bird within her hem,
    ripped the glimmering thread,
and she looked at me
as though I
had torn the moonlight in half.

Leads You to Water

Woman, I'm dreaming of you
    out there
on the desert,
    out there
at the edge of the world,
with your bare feet
padding down the dust,
your eyes grazing
the red yellow
horizon.

I send to you
the wild compass coyote,
who wanders beside you,
leads you to water leads you to water,

where I am waiting for you
to drink from my hands,
like I was like I
was the land
and you
the thirsty sky.

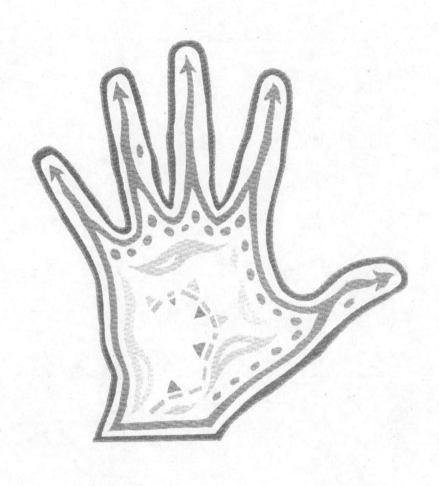

The Boy Dances

for Isaiah Drew

The boy dances around the drum. His feet rise and
fall. Sweat flies from his hair and sizzles in the
circle. His heart is a fist of blood, clenched in the
rhythm of the drum. The boy dances. His feet rise
and fall. He sees the woman standing on the edge
of the circle. The stark whiteness of her hands, the
whiteness of her face. Her eyes, the light in her eyes.

The boy dances. His feet rise and fall. His heart is
a screaming wind, a hammer. Demons fly from his
hair and flare in the circle. His feet rise and fall.
Her eyes, her eyes, the boy dances into the light of
her eyes.

Angels We

It is time to let the old Gods speak again.

It is time for the choking dust
of the old and wispy One
to be brushed away
by the wings of
new angels we.

It is time to let our shoulders rise.
It is time to let our shoulders lift.
It is time to let our shoulders open
into wings of glorious
    flame glorious.
It is time to leap
into this coming night of chaos,
once and finally,
upon wings made of pure Sun.
It is time for victory.
It is time for victory we.

Hands

Old man,
I stood over you
in your box,
and when I reached
to touch your
gray folded hands,

I remembered,
suddenly, a fair summer day
beside big water,
when you laughed
and lifted me
higher than the trees,

and I felt
like a big boy,
like a big boy,
in your hands
I felt
like a good boy,
and you said,
>   hey Chee-pwa,
>   do you see any angels up there, do you see any angels?

Old man,
I leaned over you
in your box,
touched my hands
into your
gray wave of hair,
whispered,
>   may the Grandfathers give you feathers,
>   all is forgiven
>   down here.

This Wind

All the stars
that fell last night hissing
in the wet street,
they go on burning
guiding light,
in this wind this you
that lives now forever in my hair,
forever now at the tips of my fingers.

This wind that walks
over my mouth, some spider
dancing my lips
into a silken smile,

this wind this you,
that shapes
the mountain of my face,
smoothing
away the old, jagged peaks,

this wind this you,
that laces through the lifts the
curtains
in my heart one
by one,

this wind this you,
that sees me seizes me,
carries me
warm and wildly human
through these Chicago streets,

this wind this you.

The Flower On

    If you were
the flower on
    this blanket,
resting soft upon my
    shoulder,

I would whisper
    to you (my mouth
against your petals)
of the wings
    that flutter over us
while we sleep.

Feather

for Kathleen

Long before this light,
before that first
star was ever wished
    upon,
you were a twinkle
in the universe's eye,

you were the glint
    at the tip
of a feather
on the wing
of an angel, you

are the one
that the Old Ones
came to know,
that the Old Ones
    moaned of,
scratched on walls about and,

now and here,
my hands my fingers dream
    of you,
beyond touching and,

now and here,
when I press my head
to this pillow,
your whispers rise, flutter
through my hair, your sighs
    shake
from these sheets, wash
over my belly, wash over my

hands, somehow they
remember you,
   feather,
soft alive electric,
somehow my shoulder remembers
your sleeping face and,
   darling,
I have sweet dreams.

Wedding

Our God has slept
and dreamed us here,
and from the sweat of dream
comes the sweet scent
    of vision.

We two within a northern wood,
beside a lake of morning gold,
we two before Grandfather's plume,
nestled to the breast of our new tribe.

Here upon the Earth
of my Mothers,
    I give you my eyes to see,
    I give you my hand to lead,
    I give you my breath to breathe.

Here beneath the Sky
of my Fathers,
    I give you my soul to seek,
    I give you my spirit to heal,
    I give you my heart to hold.

Together, we shall be this vision,
this water, this wood,
this Earth, this Sky.
Together, we shall be this vision,
this birth, this life, this
    eternity.

Amber On Opal

Nights,
in the heated den
of our bed,
two animals in
each other's fur,
    nips and growls and groans,
my thundering blood
drawn by your anxious claw,

become mornings,
in the cool sheets
of our bed,
man and woman,
skin to skin,
amber on opal,
    nips and growls and grins,
my happy light
drawn by your laughing flower.

Together, we make
    scent,

milk of dandelion.

Rain Rain

for Ezra Cole

Hot flashes burn
tiny holes in my one
long, cool memory.

Dreams, scenes tumble
from my hair
into the rain-slick street,
flowing streams into
the gutter,
oily rainbows
painting the feet of
ecstatic children dancing
in the puddles, singing,
 rain rain never go away,

as one small boy bends,
blows bubbles in a pool
with a straw,
laughs splashes
down the street,
glancing back at me,
dreams, scenes tumbling
from his
hair in strings
over his face.

Chippewa Hitch Hike

Hitch-hiking last night (and
    in between
the shine
    of headlights) I fell

in love with

    the moon

again.

Arrow, Humming

for Cin and Mark

I walk I run with you.
I give I take. I hide I
seek I Sun I Moon with you.
I rain I shine with you.
I flower.
I sleep I wake. I fall I rise
with you.
I laugh I weep I dark I
light with you. I pause.
I listen to your eyes.
I leap I crawl with you.
I earth I sky I sing I song
with you. I here I
now I forever with you.
I promise.

And now I know
that I always dreamed you
flying feeling
toward me, my heart
was always waiting for you.
Strong and gentle arrow,
for you my heart
was always beating,
measuring
the moment
of your arrival.

And now I know
that I always heard you
flying spinning
in my skies,
cutting through the clouds
while your feathers followed

humming
in the azure and the blue.

And now I know
that I always felt you
flying smoothing
through my nights.
Arrow, you
made the trembling
of the string
within the bending of the bow.

And now I know
that here, where we stand together,
the moment has been measured.
Arrow, you
have found me,
pierced the heart that waited,
dreaming, for you.

Arrow,
now I know your aim was true.

Motherdrum

Motherdrum motherdrum,

more than hushed
the rhythm is crushed,
muffled,
beneath the weight
of plodding footsteps,
turning wheels and smoking stacks.

Motherdrum motherdrum,

sirens kill the night,
the city
claws the stars
out of the sky,
radios
do not wave, they
eat the air,
tear the skin
from the trees.

Motherdrum motherdrum,

sirens kill the night,
the city
rapes our children,
they gang
together
in toxic alleys,
they drown in neon,
they drown in flashing signs,
seek silence
in each other's blood.

Motherdrum motherdrum,

sirens kill the night,
the city
chases away
spirits from my hair,
dreams from my reach,
hope from my eyes.

Sirens kill the night
and I cannot hear.

Ten Thousand Thousand Bones

for Joe Schranz

From long away, from
behind museum doors, from
darkly dusty rooms,

I hear Grandmother
rattling, she rattles,
among ten thousand thousand bones,
I hear Grandmother
rattling, she rattles.

She is frightened, alone,
among ten thousand thousand bones,
taken from warm belly Earth,
hot heart of Earth,
that was her resting home,

crying, cold
shaking on the shelf, alone,
    rattling,
among ten thousand thousand bones.

■   ■   ■

We wait for you Grandmother,
here in the wood,
where you belong.

The deer are stamping circles,
scratching at the ground,
leaning their ears
to listen for your song,
but you are gone.

The branches of the trees
all ache for you,
with their roots below
that once cradled you,
bending, reaching
to hear your song,
but you are gone.

The river moans
your missing voice,
the grass and stone
are silent
as they mourn
and listen listen.

The wings of hawks
call out your name and
    wonder wonder
where you've gone,

answered only by your rattling,
from where you shiver, cold,
alone,
among ten thousand thousand bones.

      ■   ■   ■

Grandmother, do not forgive
them, they know
what they have done,

taken you from
sacred circle light
and left you
in their tomb,
among all those other bones.

Fools,
they refuse to hear
the anguish in the Earth,
the cry of fox and rabbit
in your home.

Fools,
they refuse to fear
the angry step of Spirit Horse,
whose hoof
shall make a rattling
in their own living bones.

■   ■   ■

We wait for you Grandmother,
here in the wood,
where it's been so long.

The deer are scratching circles,
stamping at the ground,
leaning their ears
to listen for your song.

The branches of the trees
all ache for you,
with their roots below
that once cradled you,
reaching, bending
to hear your song.

The river moans
your missing voice,
the grass and stone
are silent
as they mourn
and listen listen.

The wings of hawks
call out your name and
    wonder wonder
where you've gone,
answered only by your rattling,
from where you shiver, cold
alone,
among ten thousand thousand bones.

Grandmother, do not forgive
them, they know
what they have done.

*From an idea by Kathleen Presnell. Dedicated to the Old One taken
from the Earth near New Lenox, Illinois in the winter of 1993-94,
and to the men and women who stood in her honor.*

Brother River Dreams

In ripples,
becoming waves,
unyielding he unchanging he
flows down,

from the woodlands
and the marshes
of northwest Ontario,
brother river dreams
and knifes his hungry way
into the fat and fleshy
heart of the places
where America is sleeping.

Brother river dreams,
glides the barren highway,
city to city,
and with his silvery, untamed teeth he
rips into the infested skins
of the factories and the machine-shops,
with his untamed teeth
into the blistered skins
of the jails and the bars,
with his untamed teeth
into the rotting skins
of the school yards,
the places
where America is sleeping.

Brother river dreams,
washes down
the canyons of Chicago,
splashes through the alleys
with the laughter of his rice-gathering People,

floods the unforgiven streets
with the blood and cries of *Anishinaabeg* ghosts,
all drowning drowning
the places
where America is sleeping.

Brother river dreams,
he speaks the fire within our veins,
he dreams, he walks, so we remain,
and his blood never forgets your shame,

So sleep on,
America,
we wake
and we are rising,
while our brother river dreams.

Cyrus Calls For His Pony

When they buried you, Cyrus,
I was ashamed
of the casket and the lid,
knowing how you dreamed
of a breathing cradle of moss and ferns,

knowing that you grumbled
and staggered to Mass,
under the heat
of your crooked suit,
only to make your woman happy.

Returning, you would dust
off your sleeves, twist your hands,
wink at us boys,
point your chin to the woods
and whisper,
    it's out there, in the trees.

Cyrus, how simply deeply
you remain with me.
Even now I smile
when I remember the last time
I saw you,

so old, so curled up
by your bones.

You pointed with your chin
to where your battered walker
leaned in the corner
and whispered,
    bring me my pony, boy, I gotta pee.

Last Drink

He thinks he
slouches at the bar,
staring down
at the last drink
in the bottom
of his glass.

He leans closer,
the dark whiskey
begins to tremble
under the
weight of his breath,
as his mind
rides the tiny ripples.

He once lived,
he thinks,
in a house
made of logs
and mud and straw,
woke in the mornings
to the sound of
dew slipping
along a blade of grass,

lived on the side
of a hill,
picked juneberries
as the soft brush
of Ojibway tongues
painted the sky,
he thinks,

remembers
the dusty grins
of sunbrown boys
chasing away the day
on tireless
stick-ponies,

his grandfather's hands,
rough and careful,
taking the skin
from a rabbit, the silver
muscle steaming
beneath
his hungry chuckle,

he thinks,
the women cooing
over baskets,
over beadwork,
over babies,
the music of them
rising higher
than the mission bells,

the summer
of the *Potawatomi* girl,
who smelled of warm bread,
fresh buttered,
under his groping mouth,
he remembers,
he once lived,

now wakes
on the street
with a chill
and the sun in his eyes,
he thinks.

Half Blood

When my brother
loves me,

he calls me
Anishinaabe,

but when he does not
love me,

he mentions
the paleness
of
my hands.

Song for the Endless Others

Mornings at my kitchen table,
drinking coffee
while the city rumbles low,
I see the Endless Others,
who live within the walls,
as they linger
in the doorways,
sit upon the window sills,
spin blade to blade,
fan to fan across the ceiling
and flutter to the floor.

When my woman curls up tight,
upon the bed,
against her breast our drowsing son,
I see the Endless Others,
who between the blankets run,
as they wrap
and as they weave
these two sleepers that I love
within soft dreams
that spread to wings and into wings,
sweeping out across the floor.

Nights, as I move about the city,
smoking Luckys,
shaking off the autumn chill,
I see the Endless Others
sparking blue beneath the El,
as they laugh
and as they dance
across the station walls,
train to train,
out into the street to tangle
up the taxis in their hair.

The Endless Others
watch my nights,
give straightness
to my crooked hands,
give me voice and give me voice,
chant and chant
within my bones.

The Endless Others
guide my days,
medicine the scars
that fill my throat,
give me voice and give me voice,
chant and chant
within my feathered heart.

The Poets Coming

for Gwendolyn Brooks

They will not be born,
instead shall fly from the mouths
   of earthen angels,
all ebony
and embered eyes,
they shall fly
from the claypot skins
of desert skies,
shall rise in light
from the forest floor,
out of the mossy river rocks,
shall rise in light.

They shall sprout from sidewalk cracks,
from pavement steam,
shall rise in light
from the factory roofs,
from the swollen belly
of the clattering city,
shall rise in light.

They shall be free to fight,
   (all fists explode into flowers),
shall rise in light
and stand to sing,
and no one again
will ever make orders
to silence the mouths from which they fly.

Growler

Once tried to kill it,

the dark animal
pacing in my chest
with all my demons
wrapped
around its tail.

I built a fire
in the back yard,
burned eighteen years
of words,
watched notebooks
curl into ash
and spiral bones.

The Growler,
writhing inside,
ripped me open,

pushed out a hesitant claw
and began to sing.

Winter

In dreamtime
it is winter
and
I lean back into a tree.

My hair is long,
silver with dusk,
my hands curled closed.

   A little wind
stirs at my shoulder,
the juice of darkness
crashes cold against my teeth,

and then
the night is gone,
and there
      is never another night.

Foreign Shore

. . . the message is coated with static
steel clutter poking into the sky
the landscape eclipsed
by the shadows of devastation . . .

Mick Vranich

The sky is
black and milky
as I rest
on this foreign shore,
   feeling
as if I'm looking down
from someplace
higher.

All along the beach
the gulls sound
   together
lifting toward the stars,
one giant wing.

This would be
the perfect night,
the perfect moment
for you to signal me
with your
ancient alien frequency.

There is no static, now.

About the author

Chippewa writer Mark Turcotte spent his earliest years on North Dakota's Turtle Mountain Reservation and in the migrant camps of the western United States. Later, he grew up in and around Lansing, Michigan. In 1993 he was the winner of the 1st Gwendolyn Brooks Open-mic Poetry Award. Most recently he has been the recipient of a Community Residency from National Writer's Voice and was awarded the 1997 Josephine Gates Kelly Memorial Fellowship from the Wordcraft Circle of Native Writers and Storytellers. The Poetry Society of America has chosen "The Flower On" for the *Poetry In Motion* project, which places poetry on public transit in certain metropolitan areas. Turcotte is also author of the collection, *Songs of Our Ancestors* (Children's Press, 1995) and a chapbook, *Road Noise* (Mesilla Press, 1998).

He lives and works in Chicago and Fish Creek, Wisconsin.

■

Inquiries:

773-866-2556 or www.contemporaryforum.com

Notes

Opening quote from *Whispering Leaves* by D.M. Demery.

Quote on page 3 from a speech by Red Cloud.

Quote on page 4 from *The Salvation of Rock* by Patti Smith.

Quote on page 20 from *Selling Shampoo* by Mike Puican.

Quote on page 26 from *End of Autumn* by Rainer Maria Rilke.

Quote on page 63 from *Famine of the Heart* by Mick Vranich.

Ojibway: originally a Great Lakes and Northern Plains people.

Crazy Horse (c.1841–1877): Oglala Lakota warrior and dreamer.

Wovoka (c.1858–1932): Paiute spiritualist who resurrected the Ghost Dance.

Nuevos amantes Indios: new Indian lovers.

Chippewa: Ojibway.

Anishinaabe(g): Ojibway name for themselves, loosely meaning "the first people."

Potawatomi: Originally a Great Lakes people.